Unlocking Unhappy

The One Tool That Set Me Free

By Michelle Edhouse CFMW

ISBN: 978-0-473-35822-8

CONTENTS

GRATITUDE

When you change something that you thought was unchangeable or "just the way that it is" the gratitude for those that have gifted you that possibility is immense. This is the gift that Access Consciousness® founder Gary Douglas and co-creator Dr. Dain Heer have gifted me with the tools of Access Consciousness®, including those in this book.

Have you ever had someone who showed you a possibility .you never knew existed? Someone who kept moving forward and creating while beckoning you to create greater too? This is the gift that Simone Milasas, author, founder and creator of Joy of Business™ has been for me.

When the world seems to be closing in on you, having someone in your life who is there for you, not judging you, allowing you to choose and create your life and still be there no matter what is a massive gift. My gratitude to Glenn, my enjoyable other, for being this for me continues and grows daily.

To all the other gifts in my life Thank YOU!!!.

UNHAPPY & SAD

So here I was plodding through life, and I say plodding – I was going a lot faster than many people I knew, but it was still not fun. It was still not joy. I was working in an area I enjoy yet at the end of the day I felt grumpy and unhappy. I would look around me and there were people who were sadder than me and there were people who were happier than me; and then there were the people I looked up to, who were just full of joy - these people were using the tools I had and creating the life they wished to live.

I asked a question. "What's it going to take to have more in my life?"

I have been an Access Consciousness® Facilitator for five years now and you would think having been a Certified Access Consciousness Facilitator, I would have used the tools on my own life, sort all my shit out and I would be happy and have loads of money.

Well – you know sometimes these areas of your life that you ignore, these areas of your life that you are not even aware aren't working for you until you clear the other shit away. And when I say shit, I am talking about the stuff you pile on top of yourself to make you look happy; the layers of paint, the layers of makeup, the layers of what you put out into the world to have the world think you're happy. :)

Are you truly happy? If you are, awesome! Put this down, turn it off, however you are listening to it. This isn't for you. If you know deep inside that there is a level of unhappiness that you would like to get rid of, I ask you to please give me a bit longer.

Now, I know the title says "The one tool" and it started with one question that I have been running; one question that I have been asking and clearing and asking and clearing. Then on top of that I have been using all the other yummy, yummy tools of Access Consciousness® and I am going to run through some of them as well as the one tool that I am going to share with you right now.

And that one question is: *"**What have you made so vital about being sad and unhappy?** "*

Yip. Sad and unhappy. Now, sad, unhappy, depressed, add whatever conditions or terminologies you use for what you're experiencing. For me, sad and unhappy. For me I wanted joy and happiness —and want means to lack (check any dictionary prior to 1940) and I did, I lacked joy, I lacked happiness.

So I was about to go in the shower one day and I asked the question "What have I made so vital about being sad and unhappy?" You could also add on the end 'that keeps me from the joy and happiness I know is true?' if you know it's possible.

But I stopped at 'What have I made so vital about being sad and unhappy?' because that was what I wanted to change. That was what I desired to change. That was what I was asking to change. There was not anything else. Just change that. Get rid of sad and unhappy and then I would have choice.

So what have you made so vital about being sad, unhappy and depressed? Everything that is, times a godzillion, will you destroy and uncreate it all? Right and wrong, good and bad, POD and POC, all nine, shorts, boys, and beyonds®.

Now for those of you who have never heard that weird wacky statement before 'Right and wrong, good and bad, POD and POC, all nine, shorts, boys, and beyonds®', it's what I like to call my magic wand from Access Consciousness®...

MY MAGIC WAND

Access Consciousness® is a set of tools and techniques that you can use to change any part of your life and living that's not working for you. And the clearing statement is one of the key elements of Access Consciousness® and you can use it like a magic wand. You ask a question, you bring up the energy of what has been going on for you and then you wave your magic wand, *'everything that is, times a godzillion, I destroy and uncreate it all. Right and wrong, good and bad, POD and POC, all nine, shorts, boys, and beyonds®.'*

Now there may be lots and lots of layers of this stuff. It may just show up at random times. There maybe bits that are hiding away and get triggered at another time that you need to clear as well. But try it. Try waving your magic wand. See what you can create. See what you can change.

Now I am not going to go into a full description of the clearing statement here because there is an absolutely awesome one on the website at www.theclearingstatement.com. So if you have never heard of it or would like more information, please go there and check it out.

So what have you made so vital about being sad, unhappy and depressed? Everything that is, times a godzillion, will you destroy and uncreate it all? Right and wrong, good and bad, POD and POC, all nine, shorts, boys, and beyonds®.

Now some of you are wondering, "so is that all she does? Is that all she asks?" No, it's not. My title, 'The one tool that set me free' was to get you to read the book. Hahaaa! But it actually was the start of me acknowledging where I was functioning from, what was going on for me; and actually being in a space where it was possible to find the other tools I could use to create the changes I was looking to create.

So - <u>what have you made so vital about being sad, unhappy and depressed? Everything that is, times a godzillion, will you destroy and uncreate it please? Right and wrong, good and bad, POD and POC, all nine, shorts, boys, and beyonds®</u>.

By asking that question over and over again and clearing the layers of muck that came up, I was able to start to see that there was stuff that I had bought, stuff that I had perceived and stuff that I had chosen, that was creating it. I was actually able to start to see what was creating what I had been experiencing, rather than just sitting in this haze of "argh!'.

What do I mean by that? Your point of view creates your reality. Some of you will have heard this before. Some of you won't. What I would like to invite you to, is how your point of view does create your reality. If you have the point of view that you're sad, depressed and unhappy, what are you going to create with that? Are you going to create being happy, being joyful? When you notice that you have that point of view, huh, cool. What can I change here? What can I do different so that I can be happy, joyful?

ALL OF LIFE COMES TO ME WITH EASE AND JOY AND GLORY!®

The next tool I would like to introduce you to, is the Access Consciousness® mantra, *'All of life comes to me with ease and joy and glory!'*. Now as I said at the beginning, I have been an Access Consciousness® Facilitator for five years. I was introduced to the tools six and a half years ago and it was one of the first tools that I was taught and yet have I been using it? No. Why not? Well because it was vital in my world to be sad, unhappy and depressed.

So if it's vital in your world to be sad, unhappy and depressed – and by vital, I mean, life sustaining. If you are not sad, unhappy and depressed, then you're not going to survive. And everything that brought up, will you destroy and uncreate it all? Right and wrong, good and bad, POD and POC, all nine, shorts, boys, and beyonds®.

If that is your point of view, will you choose to use the tool that will create ease and joy and glory? No.

So - what have you made so vital about being sad, unhappy and depressed? Everything that is, times a godzillion, will you destroy and uncreate it please? Right and wrong, good and bad, POD and POC, all nine, shorts, boys, and beyonds®.

Now, *'All of life comes to me with ease and joy and glory!'* and that mantra is actually all of life, not just the good stuff. It's '**All** of life comes to me with ease and joy and glory'. By that, if something crap happens, then, how can I deal with this with ease and joy and glory, rather than going to the sad, depressed, unhappy, woe be me, that we all have been functioning from.

So '***All of life comes to me with ease and joy and glory!***' is a tool that you can use and as I said, it's a mantra. A mantra is something that you say over and over again. What would change in your life if you were to say '***All of life comes to me with ease and joy and glory!***', ten times in the morning and ten times at night?

Would it change anything? Even just having ease and joy and glory as a possibility in your universe, what could that create? What doors could open? What questions could it create in your world?

So there is another tool for you. As I said, one tool that led to using the other tools that I am sharing with you here in this book.
'All of life comes to me with ease and joy and glory' and 'What have you made so vital about being sad, unhappy and depressed?'

In that last bit, I mentioned your point of view creates your reality. When I was talking about that, I meant to mention about all the points of view that I bought, all the points of view that I perceived. If you want to create your reality, if you buy other peoples' points of view as real and true, you make them your own. If you perceive points of view in other people, and believe they're your own, are they actually your points of view in the first place? No.

WHO DOES THIS BELONG TO?®

So this next tool, another fabulous Access Consciousness® tool, is called, 'Who does this belong to?®' Gary Douglas, the founder of Access Consciousness® says that if you were to use this tool on every thought, feeling and emotion that you have for three days, you would end up being a walking talking meditation. No thoughts in your head, just awareness. I had the chance to use this a few years ago when my father passed away suddenly and I was aware that there were going to be a lot of people with a lot of points of view and a lot of people with sadness and grief, and I chose to be me and to use this tool and to use it in a space of being able to know what was actually true for me without buying into the sadness and grief of other people.

Any time I had a thought, or a feeling, or an emotion, I asked, who does this belong to? Is it mine? Is it someone else's or is it something else's?

Now let me explain a little bit about that. Have you ever noticed that when you walk into a room you are aware of the energy of that room, or the energy of a person? That, my dear friends, is because you are psychic sponge Bob. You are aware of everything around you, whether you acknowledge it or not.

When I was growing up, to me the word psychic meant that you saw and talked to ghosts. If you didn't see them, and if you didn't talk to them and physically hear talk in your ear what they were saying, you weren't psychic. What I am now aware of is that being psychic is about being aware of what is energetically going on around you.

When you walk into a forest, do you notice a difference in the energy, than being in the centre of a hub of a bustling city? Standing next to a family in a supermarket where none of them want to be there, none of them want to be around the other person who had enough of everybody and they just wished to be alone, how do you be? What are you aware of? Are you aware of that? Do you allow it to affect you? Do you walk out of the supermarket feeling like you've just been run over by a bus? You walked in there reasonably happy and you walked out like a pile of crap.

What about when you go into a forest? You walk into the forest feeling like a pile of crap and feel it all slip away and feel an ease and a joy. Maybe for some of you, it's while you are swimming in a lake, hanging out with some cows or horses or dogs. Nature tends to be a space where people can just be. There aren't those thoughts, feelings and emotions flying at you from all directions.

What if all of life could be that kind of space? While using 'who does this belong to?' tool and a variation, which is, 'is this mine?' or 'who am I being?', you can create that space wherever you are.

I was in supermarket yesterday with my kids and I started to get grumpy with them and I started to be annoyed that they were running off with the trolley and I started to ask 'who does this belong to? Is it mine?' That lightened up. No. That felt heavy. Is it someone else's? Yeah. Ok, cool. And you don't even need to know whose it is. You don't need to lay blame. You don't need to physically pick it up and shove it back into their head. Just recognizing it's not yours, you can then choose. So do I choose to function from this anymore? Or am I choosing something else? I don't choose to function from it. Cool! Return to sender with consciousness attached. Now that is a way of putting a wedgie in the world.

What if returning all the thoughts, feelings and emotions to their sender with consciousness attached could create a greater world? What if they could have that awareness how to change what they were being if they were to choose it? That's what 'consciousness attached' does. It sends it back with the consciousness that allows them, if they choose it, to perceive what they are choosing and change it. What if it wasn't even theirs in the first place? Return to sender goes all the way back (gifting to everyone on the way) to the person who's thought feeling or emotion it was in the first place. Are you starting to see how it can change the world?

So back to the supermarket story. I was then wandering around. I could then see this family I hadn't noticed up until that point and there were five kids and an absolutely exhausted looking mother. The kids were all trying to go in different directions and they were all trying to put things in the basket that she didn't want and she didn't want to be there. They didn't want to be there. Ahh. Ok, cool. If I hadn't asked the question, who does this belong to?, I may never have even noticed them.

And you don't need to know where it comes from. Just acknowledge that it is not yours and return to sender with consciousness.

Now here's a little tip:

Sometimes when you do that, it will lighten up and feel a little bit better and then it will sink down on your shoulders again and then you return it to sender and it comes back again. And it keeps coming back. This is when you can stop and ask, ok, "Everywhere I bought this as mine, when it wasn't, I destroy and uncreate all that and return it all to sender with consciousness. Right and wrong, good and bad, POD and POC, all nine, shorts, boys, and beyonds®".

So what is that doing? If you are not really, really vigilant on asking who does this belong to, and you are like me and you grow up thinking every thought, feeling and emotion was yours, can you imagine there might be a few billion thoughts, feelings and emotions that you have experienced this lifetime that you thought were yours that weren't? As soon as you decide they are yours, what do they become? They become yours.

Dr. Dain Heer, who is the co-creator of Access Consciousness and works very closely with Gary Douglas, talks in his book "Being You, Changing The World" about his depression, his sadness and unhappiness when he first started using the Access tools. He talks about how he had this question 'who does it belong to?' taped up beside his bed on a sticky note, and he woke up one morning, his girlfriend went to work and he lay there and cried, just like most mornings. He rolled over and saw this sticky note 'who does it belong to?' and it lightened up that it wasn't his. He realized that he was aware of all of the depression going on around the world, around his area, around his suburb, around his life in general and he made that choice to not allow it to affect him. He made that choice to be him.

So could this tool be the one tool that you find changes your life?

So far, we've got, 'What have you made so vital about being sad and unhappy? Everything that is, times a godzillion, will you destroy and uncreate it please? Right and wrong, good and bad, POD and POC, all nine, shorts, boys, and beyonds®'.

Then we've got, 'All of life comes to me with ease and joy and glory'. Try that ten times in the morning and ten times at night. And 'Who does this belong to?' for every thought, feeling and emotion.

WHAT IS TRUE FOR YOU?

One of the tools that I mentioned in that last section, was light and heavy. When you ask 'Who does this belong to?', what feels light and what feels heavy? You? Someone else? Or something else? This light and heavy tool is almost like one of the rules of the universe. What's heavy and contracting is a lie for you and what's light, expansive, joyful, that sense of ahh, that sense of space that you get from the forest, that sense of space and joy when something absolutely phenomenal happens. That's the light and that's what's right for you.

There is even reference to light and heavy in the Bible. "Go to the light. Go to the light." Some people reference that when you die, you go to the light. You go to God, to whatever that be. What if it's a tool that you can use in every single moment of every single day? Go to the light. What's light? What's expansive? What's joyful for you? What if you were to choose that, rather than what's heavy and contracted and a lie for you?

<u>What have you made so vital about sad, unhappy and depressed? Everything that is, times a godzillion, will you destroy and uncreate it please? Right and wrong, good and bad, POD and POC, all nine, shorts, boys, and beyonds®.</u>
Are you starting to feel any lighter as we go through this information? Are you starting to feel more joy? More space, more ease in your world and in your body? I hope so. I certainly am as I write this.

Light and heavy. Use it. Be aware of it. When somebody asks you, "would you like to go out for coffee?" and you feel like, crikey me, that feels heavy, "um no thanks, maybe another time?"
Or, "would you like to go out for coffee?" There's a lightness and a

heaviness. Hmm. Is it go out for coffee? Yes? Now, no. What's light?

So if you were to use this light and heavy tool, I am going to call it light and heavy, you can call it space and contracted, you can call it whatever, joyful and depressing, whatever you wish to call it, but I am going to call it light and heavy because that's what we call it in Access Consciousness®.

So if you were to use this light and heavy tool in every part of your day and you were to choose the light, would that create more light and happy and joyful in your world? Or would it create heavy and contractive in your world?

I would hedge a bet that if you choose the light, it will create the light. What do you get? So would you be willing play with that? Ask, if I stop for a break now, what will that create? Oh that's light. No that's heavy, ok cool. I won't stop for a break. And then you get five minutes, if I stop for a break now, what will that create? That's really light. What were you aware of? Who knows? It may be that if you had stopped for a break five minutes ago, you would have just been getting back to work when you get a phone call that you need to pick the kids up from school because they're sick. Or it may be the phone will ring and you will be distracted and not be able to get back into your work.

Who knows what you are aware of? If you follow the light, it creates light. It creates joy. It creates expansiveness in your world.

How does it get any better than that?

What would it take for more of that to show up?

HOW DOES IT GET ANY BETTER THAN THAT?®

There's our next tool! How does it get any better than that?, is a trademark of Access Consciousness. It's a phenomenal question that you can use for everything. Why for everything? What if everything could get better and you only have to ask?

If something really grotty and horrible happens, wow, that was grotty and horrible. How does it get any better than this? So you are asking the universe, ok universe, what's it going to take to have greater than this? Something good happens. You win the lottery. Woo hoo!! How does it get any better than that? What else is possible? You're saying, this is great and can I have more please? Can I have even greater? Can I have an even bigger world than I have been having? What would it take for more of this to show up? More than this? Bigger than this?

So can you see that by asking 'How does it get any better than this?', for everything, asks for a better life, asks for a better space to live in, asks for more money, asks for more joy, more ease, more glory. Would you be willing to try that? Sometimes you might need to say it in your head because there might be some people that get really sick of hearing it, 'How does it get any better than this?', for everything. But be that question. How does it get any better than this?

My favorite shirt just ripped a hole in it. How does it get any better than this? What if asking that question allowed an even more fun, joyful, beautiful shirt to show up in your life? What if asking that question allowed you to realize that shirt was getting pretty dark and dingy and old? Because you decided it was your favorite shirt, you just didn't want to acknowledge that and then you can start to choose something greater. What? Choosing something greater? But I am not allowed!

<u>What have you made so vital about being sad, unhappy and depressed? Everything that is, times a godzillion, will you destroy and uncreate it all? Right and wrong, good and bad, POD and POC, all nine, shorts, boys, and beyonds®.</u>

OTHER PEOPLE'S POINTS OF VIEW

Dr. Dain's book, 'Being You, Changing The World', is a phenomenal book and I would highly recommend it to anybody actually wishing to create joy in their life. One of the biggest things that I got from that book and all the classes that I have done with Access, are the question of "Who am I being here? Who am I doing this for? How much of me am I shutting off in this?"

When you ask a question like that, you start to recognize all those places where you are being you, having fun, having ease, things are showing up really easy for you, and then somebody's point of view came along and you wanted to please them, you wanted to fit in with them, you wanted to be liked by them, you didn't want to be judged or rejected by them, whatever it was that you chose that for, and you cut off the joy, the ease, the being you.

Do you feel how heavy that is, cutting that off for someone else? Are you aware of what that created in your universe? Are you aware of what it is that you created as your life with that? Hmm. Downhill slide wooooo into sadness, depression, and unhappiness. So what if you were to look through your life at all the spaces where you had ease, you had joy, you had glory?

So what if you were to look at all the places that you were being you, you were being happy? Life was just cruising along, happy and joyful and ease? You would ask for something and it would show up. Everything was just working for you THEN somebody judged you. Somebody made a comment. Somebody sneered. Somebody said "oh it can't be that easy" or "why are you so happy? What drug are you on?" and you shut it down.

What points of view do you have that create that? That you need to fit in? That you need to be the same as everybody else? You need to be liked? You don't wish to be judged? What points of view do you have underlying all that, that creates you shutting off you for other people? <u>Everything that is, times a godzillion, will you destroy and uncreate it all? Right and wrong, good and bad, POD and POC, all nine, shorts, boys, and beyonds®.</u>

You know there are some people out there who have decided if you are in a family, you have to be like your family. And if your family is sad and depressed, what do you have to create you as, to be like your family?

How many times do you get "wow you look like your mum" or "you're just like your dad" and if you buy that point of view, and if your mum or dad are not happy, what do you have to create you as? You have to create you as unhappy? <u>Everything that is and everywhere you have done that, would you be willing destroy and uncreate all that? Right and wrong, good and bad, POD and POC, all nine, shorts, boys, and beyonds®.</u>

<u>What have you made so vital about being sad, unhappy and depressed? Everything that is, times a godzillion, will you destroy and uncreate it all? Right and wrong, good and bad, POD and POC, all nine, shorts, boys, and beyonds®.</u>

So who are you being when you are sad or unhappy? About 90% of the population maybe? I am not asking you to blame anyone for your sadness because it's your choice to duplicate them, to be like them, to cut you off to be like them.

What if you were to look at it and go "huh, who am I being here? Me or someone else?" You don't have to decide who it is. You don't have to go "oh I am trying to be like my mother" or "oh I am trying to be like my brother" or "oh I am trying to be like Sarah Jane who I went to school with when I was eight." You just have to acknowledge who you are being, you or someone else?

Again, ask the question, use the awareness of the light and heavy, and then choose, who would I like to be?

So, any time you are feeling sad or unhappy or depressed or all three, ask, 'Who am I being here? Me or someone else?" If it lightens up on someone else, ok, "What energy, space and consciousness can I be to be me with total ease?"

What energy, space and consciousness can I be to be me with total ease?

"What is me?", I hear you ask. "Who am I, if I am not these thoughts and feelings and emotions that I am getting from everyone else, if I am not all those things I have decided I must be to fit in with everybody. Who am I?" That's a great, great question. If you have no point of view about who you are, who would you like to be in these ten seconds? What if you being you was a ten second choice?

Another fabulous tool from Access Consciousness — ten second increments.

10 SECOND CHOICE

What if no choice was the wrong choice? What if no choice was the right choice? What if it were just A choice? And with it being just a choice, you can choose again and then choose again.

If you were choosing your life right now would you choose to be happy or sad? Will you be that now for 10 seconds? 1.2.3.4.5.6.7.8.9.10 Now choose again.
If you were choosing your life right now would you choose to be happy or sad? Will you be that now for 10 seconds? 1.2.3.4.5.6.7.8.9.10 Now choose again.

You can choose to keep creating the same thing or you can choose something else. Happy. Sad. Sad. Happy. Sad. Happy. Happy. Happy. Sad.

What energy, space and consciousness can I be? A new ten seconds. What energy, space and consciousness can I be?

What if every ten seconds was different and what if there were a whole group of ten seconds' that you chose to be the same as the previous ten seconds? And then, what if there were no solidity, 'well this is who I am', and change is just a choice? Is there anything you have decided is you that if you are not being it, you are not being you? Would you be willing to let that go? What if you being you was a choice in every ten seconds and what that looked like could change in every ten seconds? Would that bring more ease, more joy, more glory?

All of life comes to me with ease and joy and glory.

If you are functioning in ten second increments of who you be and how you be and it is not ease joy and glory ask: Who am I being? Me or someone else? Someone else. <u>What energy, space and consciousness can I be to be me with total ease? Everything that doesn't allow that, will you destroy and uncreate it all? Right and wrong, good and bad, POD and POC, all nine, shorts, boys, and beyonds®.</u>

GET YOUR BARS RUN!

One of the places that I have been is that space of "I can't change this, I can't think, my brain is mush, nothing seems to be possible, and everything I try fails, everything I do fails" and there is a tool for this!
And it doesn't require you to do anything other than book an appointment.

What am I talking about? I am talking about Access Bars®. Access Bars have cleared the space in my head to be me and to have choice again so many times I have lost count. I always know that I require my bars run when I get to that space of nothing is possible.

So what are The Bars? What are these weird things she is talking about and how do I get an appointment and all of that stuff?
Access Bars are these energetic bars in your head that is where you store the energetic component of all the thoughts feelings and emotions that you have in this and any other lifetime. The way I picture them is a bit like arteries and as they gather bits of thoughts feelings and emotions they start to clog up. When the energy can't flow through those bars anymore is when you be in that space of mush, where there is so much going on, it's like there are voices that won't shut up and nothing seems to be clear.

So having your bars run is a very simple process, you find an Access Bars facilitator or practitioner and you lay down on their table and get them to put their hands on your head. And that's it!

A full session is usually 1 to 1.5 hours long, you can have quick top up sessions; but if you get to that mushy head space I would go for a full session.

Literally they (the facilitator or practitioner) just lightly touch the energetic points on your head and allow all that clogged up stuff to flow out, to dissipate, to disappear. What you end up with is a space of ease and joy and possibility. Having taught a number of people the Bars and received the Bars from a range of people, what I have received from each session is different but every session I have a different space, lighter and more ease.

So if nothing else in this book is working and you just require someone else to contribute to changing it **Get Your Bars Run!!**

Even if you don't get to that space, getting your Bars run is such a contribution. My target is to get my bars run once a week whether I "need" them run or not. It is such a gift and contribution to you and your body and I have never found anything else that can create what having your Bars run can.

Find a facilitator or practitioner on www.bars.accessconsciousness.com

CAN YOU USE THESE TOOLS?

So are these tools that you could perhaps use?
Simple tools that are easy to use?
I invite you to use them.
I invite you to play with them.

If you find them useful, if you find them easeful, I invite you to explore more tools from www.AccessConsciousness.com. There are facilitators all around the world of which I and my husband are two of them from all around the world, there's psychiatrists, there's psychologists, there's all sorts of people in all sorts of professions that teach these tools & offer private sessions for you to clear stuff.

There are some facilitators who use these tools in different areas of specialty. Some that relate to this book's topic are:

Marilyn Bradford in the United States who teaches 'Right Recovery For You', recovery from addiction. One of the major addictions she talks about is addiction to the wrongness of you. Is that something you have been using to create sadness, the depression and unhappiness? What if you are not wrong? Woooo. That's a biggie and I am not going to go into that here but if you are interested in it, check out 'Right Recovery For You'.

Then there's the book and classes by Susanna Mittermaier, who is a clinical psychologist, and that's called 'Pragmatic Psychology' and the byline is "Practical tools for being crazy happy".
Crazy happy! Now that sounds a bit weird to me. Crazy happy is definitely something that this reality, this society doesn't encourage. A - being crazy is wrong! And B - being happy is weird! Maybe that's your next step. ;)

So have a look around. There are classes and books and there are private sessions.
And there's you!
Maybe these tools and this book are all that you actually require. Maybe just using these tools, or just one of these tools can change your life. Use them. Just like any other tool – hammer, a saw, if you buy it and leave it in its box, it's not going to build you a house. It's not going to cut up your firewood.
Choose to try a tool.
Use all of them.
Jump in with both feet and do lots of classes.
Or none of the above.
It's all your choice.
It's also your choice to stay sad, depressed and unhappy. Gary Douglas and Dr. Dain have even done a class called 'Happiness is just a choice' and it was the least attended class they have ever done.

What choice are you making?
Choice trumps all.

So one last question you may choose to ask yourself:

<u>What have you made so vital, valuable and real about being sad, depressed and unhappy that keeps you from choosing and creating the life and living you desire? Everything that is will you now destroy and uncreate it all? Right and wrong, good and bad, POD and POC, all nine, shorts, boys, and beyonds®.</u>

ABOUT THE AUTHOR

Michelle Edhouse best describes herself as a facilitator of change. Empowering people to quit life-long drug addiction through to conceiving a child after months of trying Michelle's CFMW status is well documented. Drawing on life experiences ranging from student activism to office management as well as developing her talents as an artist and website creator, she is well aware that the possibilities are infinite if we choose them.

Michelle always thought of herself as a normal middle class girl with an engineering/mathematical brain. Michelle studied Computer Science, Mathematics and Management Systems at University but she always knew there was more available than what she saw those around her choosing.

Having used the tools of Access Consciousness in her own life, she enjoys helping those that wish to create more. Her own changes have been subtle in some areas but profound in others. *This ease I have with my children now is something I could never have imagined possible.* The tools and techniques in Access have also opened up possibilities in business (www.WWWebsites.co.nz) and creativity (www.McEArt.co.nz) by clearing out limitations and asking "What else is possible here?"

Based in Rotorua, New Zealand Michelle lives with her husband Glenn and two sons. She travels the world facilitating classes and offers private sessions in person and online.

Find out more at www.AccessYou.co.nz/michelle-edhouse